Building an Effective Prayer Life

Antonio M. Palmer

Building an Effective Prayer Life

Copyright © 2017 by Antonio M. Palmer

Revised 2022

ISBN 978-1-947741-03-4

Published by Kingdom Publishing, LLC
1350 Blair Drive, Suite F, Odenton, MD 21113
Printed in the USA

All rights reserved. No part of this book may be reproduced, stored in a retrieval system, or transmitted in any form or by any means – electronic, mechanical, photocopy, recording, or otherwise – except for brief quotations in printed reviews, without the prior written permission of the author.

Unless otherwise indicated, all Scripture quotations are taken from the New King James Version, copyright © 1979, 1980, 1982 by Thomas Nelson, Inc. Publishers. Scripture quotations noted KJV are from the King James Version. Scripture quotations noted NIV are from the Holy Bible: New International Version® Copyright © 1973, 1978, 1984 by International Bible Society. Used by permission of Zondervan Publishing House. All rights reserved. Scripture quotations noted NLT are from the Holy Bible, New Living Translation, copyright © 1996. Used by permission of Tyndale House Publishers, Inc. Wheaton, Illinois 60189. All rights reserved. Scripture quotations noted NASB are from the New American Standard Bible ®, copyright © the Lockman Foundation 1960, 1962, 1963, 1968, 1971, 1972, 1973, 1975, 1977. Used by permission. Scripture quotations noted AMPLIFIED or AMP are taken from the Amplified ® Bible, copyright © 1954, 1958, 1962, 1964, 1965, 1987 by the Lockman Foundation. Used by permission (www.Lockman.org). Scripture quotations noted The Complete Jewish Bible are taken from The Complete Jewish Bible, copyright © 1998 by David H. Stern. Published by Jewish New Testament Publication, Inc. www.messianicjewish.net/jntp. Distributed by Messianic Jewish Resources. www.messianicjewish.net. All rights reserved. Used by permission. Scripture quotations noted The Message Bible are from The Message Bible. Copyright © 1993, 1994, 1995, 1996, 2000, 2001, 2002. Used by permission of NavPress Publishing Group

This book is dedicated to my grandmother, Mama Rose Roberson.

Table of Contents

Introduction
1

Chapter 1
What is Prayer?
5

Chapter 2
Three Key Benefits of Prayer
9

Chapter 3
Acceptable Prayer
11

Chapter 4
Why We Need to Pray
17

Chapter 5
Why We Don't Pray
21

Chapter 6
Hindrances to Answered Prayers
23

Chapter 7
The Model Prayer of Jesus
27

Chapter 8
Effective Praying
33

Chapter 9
Praying in the Holy Ghost
51

Conclusion
59

About the Author

61

Introduction

If there is ever a time for believers to bombard heaven in prayer it is now. I sincerely believe that our spiritual growth is stunted without daily meaningful communication with our heavenly Father. Jesus declared that men should always pray and not lose heart (give up). A growing, maturing prayer life will move the hand of God.

Powerful results have come from men who prayed fervently. The nation of Israel prayed for freedom from Egyptian bondage and God answered them by sending them a deliverer whose name was Moses. Joshua prayed and the sun stood still, giving them more daylight time to complete their destruction upon their enemy. Hannah, who was barren, prayed and gave birth to a son (Samuel) who became a great prophet to Israel. Daniel prayed and the mouths of lions were shut up. Elijah prayed and the heavens gave no rain for three and half years. Jesus[1], Peter and Paul prayed and there were many miracles that took place through their ministry. Many modern believers have prayed and produced God-kind of results. The Apostle James tells us that Elijah was a mere man just like us. He underwent difficulties and temptations like us, nevertheless he moved the hand of God by prayer. This lets us know that if we build the habit of prayer then we, too, can move the hand of God and produce God-kind of results.

---

[1] Jesus is the English name used to translate His actual Hebrew name, Yeshua (or Yahusha). We will simply reference the name Jesus in this book because it is more commonly used in the Western church.

I believe the Lord is issuing a clarion call to the church to pray like never before. It is the same call that He voiced in Solomon's day,

"If My people who are called by My name will humble themselves, and pray and seek My face, and turn from their wicked ways, then I will hear from heaven, and will forgive their sin and heal their land" (2 Chronicles 7:14 NKJV).

In this trumpeted call of God, He instructs us to do four things that will get His attention and a favorable response. These four things are:

1. Humble ourselves
2. Pray
3. Seek His face
4. Turn from our wicked ways

The favorable response that we will receive from the Lord is threefold:

1. He will hear from heaven
2. He will forgive us of our sin and
3. He will heal our land

The purpose of this book is to help build a prayer focus for the people of God. As you read through this book, you will gain an understanding of prayer and know its importance. Ideally, we do not want you to just learn about prayer but to literally get into the habit of praying. Communicating with God should be the believer's highest priority.

In this book, you will be equipped on how to pray effectively, and you will grow in the word of God concerning prayer by learning key, relevant scriptures on prayer, the reason why we

Introduction

should pray, hindrances to praying, and how to pray effectively – getting results.

Chapter 1
What is Prayer?

In this chapter we will define what prayer means by giving you the dictionary definition along with the biblical words that were used for prayer, and what these words mean. First, we will look at the dictionary definitions:

1. The Miriam-Webster's Dictionary defines prayer as *an address such as a petition to God or a god in word or thought.*
2. The British Dictionary (cited on Dictionary.com) defines prayer as *a personal communication or petition addressed to a deity, especially in the form of supplication, adoration, praise, contrition, or thanksgiving or any form of spiritual communion to a deity.*
3. The Easton's Bible Dictionary says that prayer is *conversation with God; the intercourse of the soul with God; not in contemplation or meditation, but in direct address to Him.* It is "beseeching the Lord" (Exodus 32:11), "pouring out the soul before the Lord" (1 Samuel 1:15), and "drawing near to God" (Psalm 73:28).

We first see God communicating with Man [Adam] in the garden of Eden in Genesis 3:8, *"And they heard the voice of the Lord walking in the cool of the day..."* and after Adam hid himself from God because of his disobedience, God calls for the man, "Adam, where art thou?" The first man, Adam, heard God's voice and responded to him. From the onset, man had the ability to communicate with God. He created us to be able to communicate with us. He is a communicable God.

Prayer is a two-way conversation with God. It is communion with Him which involves intimate communication.

After the fall of Man, we see prayer enacted in Genesis 4:26, "And as for Seth, to him also a son was born; and he named him Enosh. Then men began *to call on* the name of the Lord."

In the New Testament there are several Greek words that are translated as prayer such as *deomai, eratao, euchomai, parakaleo, proseuche (proseuchomai)* and *aiteo*. Let's define each word:

1. Deomai means "to beseech, to want/lack, to desire, long for, ask, beg, pray or make supplication."
2. Eratao means "to question, to ask, to request, entreat, beg, beseech."
3. Euchomai means "to pray or to pray for; to wish."
4. Parakaleo means "to call to one's side, to call for, to summon, to address, to speak to, to call upon, to beg, entreat or beseech."
5. Proseuche means "prayer addressed to God; a place set apart or suited for the offering of prayer." (Proseuchomai simply means to offer prayers)
6. Aiteo means "to ask, beg, call for, crave, desire, require, or make a request."

From these New Testament words for prayer, we have a collective meaning for prayer. It means "to beseech, ask, beg, entreat, call to one's side, address, speak to, call upon or make a request." Also, from these New Testament words we can say that prayer is often

Chapter 1 - What is Prayer?

produced from a heart that craves for, longs for, or desires God and his will to be done and for needs to be fulfilled. You will rarely pray for something you do not desire.

The key word for prayer is *beseech*. Beseech actually means "to petition God, to implore urgently; to beg earnestly for; to supplicate." I can vouch for this definition because usually when I request something from God it requires his immediate attention so I call on Him urgently. And trust me, it is also something I desire or something I feel needs to be fulfilled. Beseeching prayer is an earnest plea. It is sincere, deep and intense – just like God wants it. Prayer is intense. God isn't into dull moments or dull relationships and you shouldn't be either.

This leads to my main point about prayer. It should never be done out of religious obligation, but always from a relational perspective, i.e., your personal relationship with the Father.

Chapter 2
Three Key Benefits of Prayer

Dr. David Yonggi Cho, pastor of the largest church in the world, said in his book, Prayer that Brings Revival,

> "God has created us in such a way that we need to know the purpose and benefit of something if we are going to be motivated to work for that thing. If we actually knew the benefits of prayer, we would have been praying by now. Motivation works on the basis of desire. For someone to pray, he must learn to desire prayer. How can you develop the desire to pray? You must see the eternal and temporal benefits of prayer."

He goes on to talk about three unique benefits of prayer. I'd like to briefly discuss these three benefits hoping that it will spark a desire in you to pray. The three benefits that Dr. Cho shares in his book are *power, brokenness,* and *authority to overcome Satan and evil.*

PRAYER PRODUCES POWER

To develop power in prayer we must change our attitude about prayer. In the gospel according to Matthew, Jesus made a revolutionary statement regarding the attitude necessary to produce spiritual power.

Building an Effective Prayer Life

> *"Verily I say unto you, among them that are born of women there hath not risen a greater than John the Baptist; notwithstanding he that is least in the kingdom of heaven is greater than he. And from the days of John the Baptist until now the kingdom of heaven suffereth violence, and the violent take it by force"* (Matthew 11:11-12).

The attitude that Jesus states here for prayer is an attitude of violence. Adam Clarke called the violence that Jesus referred to as *"the required violent earnestness."* Violence means *intense in force.* The violent are those who, like a hurricane, will destroy anything in their path that will interrupt or hinder their sincere devotion to God. It will take a violent dedication to prayer to bring the power of God into our lives. This violent earnestness or dedication will be most evident in our discipline. Power in prayer takes much time. For this reason, we must set priorities for our time. This is why Corrie ten Boom said,

> *"Don't pray when you feel like it. Have an appointment with the Lord and keep it. A man is powerful on his knees."*

Revivalist John Wesley says,

> *"God does nothing except in response to believing prayer."*

Chapter 2 - Three Key Benefits of Prayer

    In fact, if we never pray, God is not obligated to do anything for us. When we pray, God cannot deny Himself. The very reason why there were so many miracles in the ministry of Jesus and in the early church is because of prayer. The reason why there is little or limited power in today's church is simply because of the lack of prayer. I remember what Archbishop Nicholas Duncan-Williams, nicknamed "the apostle of prayer," says about the church's lack of prayer, calling it an epidemic. He labeled this epidemic as the PWC virus or Prayerlessness-Without-Ceasing virus. We must pray with violent earnestness if we are going to seize the kingdom of heaven and release God's power.

    Prayer produces power, and we should be motivated by the fact that God desires to use us to demonstrate His awesome power. However, He only demonstrates His power in answer to believing prayer. His power should give you a desire to pray.

    S. D. Gordon gave an awesome quote about prayer. He said, "The great people of the earth today are the people who pray! I do not mean those who talk about prayer, or those who say they believe in prayer, or those who explain prayer, but I mean those who actually take the time to pray. They have no time. It must be taken from something else. That something else is important, very important, and pressing, but still, less important and pressing than prayer. There are people who put prayer first and group the other items in life's schedule around and after prayer. These are the people today who are doing the most for God in winning souls, in solving problems, in awakening churches, in supplying both men and money for mission posts, in keeping fresh and strong their lives far off in sacrificial service on the foreign field, where the thickest fighting is going on, and in keeping the old earth sweet a little while longer."

E. M. Bounds made the great statement,

"Real prayer is not learned in a classroom but in the closet."

If you're reading this book, you, my friend, have the awesome privilege to begin a life of prayer that can produce the kind of power that will shape tomorrow's world.

PRAYER BRINGS BROKENNESS

God cannot fully use a person who is not broken and completely surrendered to Him. If there is anyone who knows something about brokenness, it is the apostle Peter. He first encounters Jesus at the dawn of an unsuccessful fishing trip. With a boat full of empty nets and ice coolers, the rugged fisherman was overly frustrated and probably verbalizing his frustrations with vulgar outbursts. After all, he was known as a "curser." Jesus came early in the morning while Peter was basically washing his nets, perhaps gathering his work gear, and calling it a day. He makes one request of Peter to get back in the boat and let down his net one more time. When Peter finally agreed to do so, his net and his coworkers' nets caught so many fish that their nets began to tear! It was only when Peter realized what had happened that he fell to his knees before Jesus and said, "Oh, Lord, please leave me – I'm such a sinful man." He was broken by the evidence of God's power and love for him.

Chapter 2 - Three Key Benefits of Prayer

Another incident involving Peter was his denial of Jesus three times. When he realized that his fear led him to denying his Master, remembering Jesus' prophetic words to him about denying three times that he ever knew him before the cock crowed in the morning, he became saddened and despondent. He became broken by this. When Jesus rose from the dead, He went straight to Peter and restored Him with forgiveness and grace. Then He instructed him to feed His sheep. Out of his brokenness, God used Peter to preach on the day of Pentecost, and three thousand people came to Christ on that very day!

Brokenness is accomplished through prayer. Prayer is all about encountering God. Usually, when you come into contact with God in your prayer time, the first thing you feel in your heart as you enter into His presence is a realization of your sin, like Peter. Then you begin to confess your sin and humble yourself before Him. That's the proper response. Abiding in His presence will produce brokenness and submission. Brokenness gives us a humbling awareness of our own unworthiness as sinners and of our own insignificance as powerless creatures before an omnipotent God. This ultimately leads us to unhesitatingly submit to the divine will of God.

There isn't anything God desires more than to find a person with a broken heart who He can restore and use mightily. Your pain, your grief, and your trials were meant to bring you closer to God. He is so near to us when we respond in total surrender to Him.

"The Lord is near to those who have a broken heart and saves such as have a contrite spirit" (Psalm 34:18).

Brokenness not only causes surrender to God but also a dependence upon Him. For God to do something mighty in and through us, it is going to take a dependence upon Him. We must rely on the character, power and great name of our God. He has a great track record of helping His people. Knowing that God greatly uses people who are broken, surrendered and dependent upon Him, we should have a burning desire to pray.

PRAYER GIVES US AUTHORITY TO OVERCOME SATAN AND EVIL

Samuel Chadwick says, "The one concern of the devil is to keep Christians from praying. He fears nothing from prayerless studies, prayerless work, and prayerless religion. He laughs at our toil, mocks at our wisdom, but he trembles when we pray."
William Cowper quotes,

"Satan trembles when he sees the weakest Christian on his knees."

Jesus has given us authority over the works of the devil:

"Behold, I give unto you *power* to tread on serpents and scorpions, and over all the power of the enemy: and nothing shall by any means hurt you" (Luke 10:18, emphasis added).

The Greek word translated as *"power"* in the above scripture is *exousia*, which is better rendered as "authority". Its meaning is "the right to exercise power." Jesus is telling his disciples that He

Chapter 2 - Three Key Benefits of Prayer

has given us the right to exercise Kingdom power to disrupt, overcome, and overthrow all the evil works of Satan and his cohorts. This is the benefit of communicating with God – nothing shall by any means hurt you. You should cause damage to the enemy's kingdom, not the other way around.

Chapter 3
Acceptable Prayer

"I would rather teach one man to pray than ten men to preach."
Charles Spurgeon

All so often when new converts come to Christ they are encouraged to pray. That encouragement is no more than someone telling them to pray or come to a scheduled prayer meeting at the church. Simply put, they were *told* to pray and not *taught* how to pray. Both Jesus and John the baptizer taught their disciples how to pray (Luke 11:1). Prayer is teachable.

To begin developing an effective prayer life, you would want to know what makes prayer acceptable to God. There are specific things in Scripture that reveal to us what must be woven into the fabric of our prayers to God. Here are nine key components that make prayer acceptable to God:

1. Acceptable prayer must be done in faith (Matthew 21:22).
2. Acceptable prayer must be from a sincere heart (Hebrews 10:22).
3. Acceptable prayer must be done with the right motive (James 4:3).
4. Acceptable prayer must be done in the name of Jesus (John 15:16; 16:23-24; Ephesians 5:20; Colossians 3:17).
5. We should not pray as the hypocrites (Matthew 6:5).
    a. Hypocrites love praying standing in the synagogues
    b. Hypocrites love being seen of men

       c. Hypocrites used vain repetition and much speaking
6. Acceptable prayer is made by the righteous (James 5:16).
7. Acceptable prayer is praying with forgiveness
   (Matthew 6:14-15).
8. Acceptable prayer is praying without giving up (Luke 18:1).
9. Acceptable prayer is praying according to His will
   (1 John 5:14).

Chapter 4
Why We Need to Pray

Where the church is advancing around the world, people are praying.

"Be anxious for nothing, but in everything by prayer and supplication with thanksgiving let your requests be made known to God" (Philippians 4:6).

One of the biggest questions that some people would ask concerning prayer is "Why pray?" They may say, "What is the point of praying when God knows the future and is already in control of everything? If we cannot change His mind, why should we pray?"

Remember, the very definition of prayer involves intimate communion and conversation with God. Thus, when we pray, we are ultimately inviting God into our lives – hopefully every day. He desires unhindered, unbroken fellowship with us. Prayer does not change God's mind, but it changes our mind. Here are some reasons why we need to pray:

1. Prayer is a form of serving God (Luke 2:36-38) and obeying Him.
2. We pray because God commands us to pray (Luke 18:1; Philippians 4:6-7; 1 Thessalonians 5:17).
3. Prayer is exemplified for us by Jesus and the early church (Mark 1:35; Acts 1:14; 2:42; 3:1; 4:23-31; 6:4; 13:1-3). Think about it – if Jesus thought it was worthwhile to pray,

we should also. If He needed to pray to remain in the Father's will, how much more do we need to pray?
4. Another reason to pray is that God intends prayer to be the means of obtaining His solutions in a number of situations.
   a. We pray in preparation for major decisions (Luke 6:12-13).
   b. We pray to overcome demonic barriers (Matthew 17:14-21).
   c. We prayer to gather workers for the spiritual harvest (Luke 10:2).
   d. We pray to gain strength to overcome temptation (Matthew 26:41) and
   e. We pray to obtain the means of strengthening others spiritually (Ephesians 6:18-19).
5. We have God's promise that our prayers are not in vain even if we do not receive specifically what we ask for (Matthew 6:6; Romans 8:26, 27).
   a. He has promised that when we ask for things that are in accordance to His will, He will give us what we ask for (1 John 5:14-15).
   b. Sometimes He delays His answers according to His wisdom and for our benefit. In these situations, we are to be diligent and persistent in prayer (Matthew 7:7; Luke 18:1-8).
   c. Prayer should not be seen as our means of getting God to do our will on earth, but rather as a means of getting God's will done on earth.
   d. For situations in which we do not know God's will specifically, prayer is a means of discerning His will.

Chapter 4 - Why We Need to Pray

6. A lack of prayer demonstrates a lack of faith and a lack of trust in God's word. We pray to demonstrate our faith in God, that He will do as He has promised in His word and bless our lives abundantly, more than we could ask or imagine (Ephesians 3:20).
7. When righteous people pray they can accomplish much (James 5:16).
8. Through prayer, we align ourselves with the Spirit (Romans 8:25-26).
9. Through prayer, we yield to the lordship of Christ.
10. Through prayer, we learn to recognize the voice of the Shepherd.
11. We pray to receive mercy and grace to help us in our time of need (Hebrews 4:16).
12. We pray to focus on God and not our circumstances (Psalm 77:1-12; Philippians 4:6).

Chapter 5
Why We Don't Pray

"We have not, because we ask not."
James 4:1

"God forbid that I should sin against the Lord in ceasing to pray for you."
1 Samuel 12:23

There are several reasons why we do not pray. Here are some:

1. Some people don't look at it as sin when we do not pray. But Samuel said he'd be sinning or offending the Lord if he didn't pray.
2. Some people feel there is no need to pray.
3. Some people feel they have no time to pray – they are just too busy. It's not that they don't have time; they just don't make it a priority, and therefore, time escapes them. We always make time for what we treasure.
4. Some people simply don't know how to pray, or they have never been taught how to pray.
5. Some people feel they have too much sin in their lives and therefore, they are not good enough for God, or that He is too angry at them.
6. Some people feel that prayer is just too boring.
7. Some people may feel their situation is too hopeless and see no need to pray.

8. Some people feel that they just don't know where to begin, so they never end up beginning at all.
9. Some people doubt God hears them.
10. Some people feel they will receive something different than what they ask for (in a negative way).
11. Some people don't pray because they simply don't feel like praying.
12. Some people don't pray because they don't want anything from God (as though they are content with life and don't want to disturb God with menial stuff).
13. Some people don't pray because they don't care enough about others.

Chapter 6
Hindrances to Answered Prayers

"What is the source of quarrels and conflicts among you? Is not the source your pleasures that wage war in your members? You lust and do not have; so you commit murder. You are envious and cannot obtain; so you fight and quarrel. You do not have because you do not ask. You ask and do not receive, because you ask with wrong motives, so that you may spend it on your pleasures."
James 4:1-3

When asked how much time he spent in prayer, George Muller's reply was, "Hours every day. But I live in the spirit of prayer, I pray as I walk and when I lie down and when I arise. And the answers are always coming."

Our God is a prayer answering God. He says emphatically, *"Call unto me and I will answer thee, and shew thee great and mightily things, which thou knowest not"* (Jeremiah 33:3). When we pray God promises to respond to us.

Elijah had known Him to answer by fire, "Then the fire of the Lord fell and consumed the burnt offering and the wood and the stones and the dust, and licked up the water that was in the trench" (1 Kings 18:38 NASB). Aaron and Moses, David and Solomon each experienced God answering by fire as He consumed their sacrificial offerings dedicated to Him. He will answer you when you call upon Him in faith. In Psalm 91:14-15, God explicitly says that He will deliver those who love Him; set them on high and whenever they *"call upon Me and I will answer"* (Psalm 91:14, 15).

Although our God desires so much to answer our prayers, there are a couple of things that hinder us from receiving answers to prayers. They are:

1. <u>Selfishness</u>. James 4:3 says that we ask and receive not because we ask amiss, that we may spend it in our pleasures. Selfish people ask God for stuff with the intent of receiving from Him so that they can spend it in their pleasures.

2. <u>Sin</u>. Isaiah 59:1, 2 says that the Lord's hand is not shortened that it cannot save or His ear heavy that it cannot hear, but our iniquities have separated us from God and our sins have hid His face from us that "He will not hear."

3. <u>A Condemned Heart</u>. 1 John 3:20-22 says, "If our hearts know something against us, God is greater than our hearts and He knows everything…if our hearts know nothing against us, we have confidence in approaching God; then whatever we ask for we receive from Him."

4. <u>Idolatry</u>. In Ezekiel 14:3, God asks the prophet a serious question, "Son of man, these men have taken their idols into their heart…should I be inquired of (called upon or prayed to) at all by them?" The Lord was basically refusing to listen to the prayers of those who had idols endeared in their hearts. He'd rather they pray to those foolish idols than to Him. Idolatry is a serious offense to God. He warned His people that He was a jealous God and that He did not want them to serve any other gods beside Him.

Chapter 6 - Hindrances to Answered Prayers

5. <u>Stinginess</u>. God has a special love for those who are poor, and the Bible even tells us that His eye is upon them, insomuch that their poverty draws His special attention. In fact, the first reason why Jesus said that the Spirit of the Lord anointed Him was to preach the gospel to the poor. In Proverbs 21:13, God's heart toward the poor is revealed: "Whoso stoppeth his ear at the cry of the poor, he also shall cry himself, but shall not be heard." God blesses those who care for the poor and needy, but He won't even entertain the prayers of those who ignore their concerns and needs.

6. <u>Unforgiveness</u>. Mark 11:25 declares, *"And when ye stand praying, forgive, if ye have ought against any; that your father also which is in heaven may forgive you your trespasses."* An unforgiving spirit is one of the most subtle but most common hindrances to prayer. Our very first prayer that God answered was one of repentance, where God forgave us of all the wrongdoings that we committed against Him and others. In return, He made it a requirement that we stand forgiving others if we are to commune with Him. Anyone who is nursing a grudge against another has closed the ear of God against his own petition.

7. <u>Spousal Disunity</u>. A wrong relation between husband and wife is a hindrance to prayer. "Ye husbands, in like manner, dwell with your wives according to knowledge, giving honor unto the woman, as the weaker vessel, as being also joint-heirs of the grace of life; to the end that your prayers be not hindered" (1 Peter 3:7).

8. <u>Doubt</u>. The final hindrance to prayer is found in James 1:5-7. It says, *"But if any of you lacketh wisdom, let him ask of God, who giveth to all liberally and upbraideth not; and it shall be given him. But let him ask in faith, nothing doubting: for he that doubteth*

is like the surge of the sea driven by the wind and tossed. For let not that man think that he shall receive anything of the Lord." The apostle James warns us that we should not even think that we're going to receive anything from the Lord if we pray doubting. We must pray in faith and not in doubt.

Chapter 7
The Model Prayer of Jesus

Since Jesus taught His disciples how to pray and prayer is teachable, we will use "The Lord's Prayer" as our starting point for building a life of prayer (this was Jesus' disciples' starting point as well). When I first began to pray, I learned and recited the Lord's Prayer. Once I understood why Jesus prayed these specific prayer points, it helped me build my own conversation with the Father, using this prayer as my foundation. The Lord's Prayer (or The Model Prayer) is found in Matthew 6:9-13:

> *"After this manner therefore pray ye: our father which art in heaven, hallowed be thy name. Thy kingdom come. Thy will be done in earth, as it is in heaven. Give us this day our daily bread. And forgive us our debts, as we forgive our debtors. And lead us not into temptation, but deliver us from evil. For thine is the kingdom, and the power, and the glory, forever. Amen."*

In this model prayer Jesus makes eight essential points which I will briefly discuss.

<u>Prayer Point 1</u>: Jesus started teaching His disciples how to pray by first saying, "Our Father (which art in heaven)." By addressing God as Father, Jesus was showing that first and foremost prayer is all about an intimate, personal relationship between a father and his child. We must become acquainted with God as our father,

and we, His children. He is Abba, Life-giver, Creator, Source, Sustainer, Provider, etc. He is called "Father of lights" in James 1:17 and "Father of mercies" in 2 Corinthians 1:3. We are to have childlike faith, and our prayers should always be like a child coming to talk to his father. Prayer should always begin with knowing that you are addressing your Father (in heaven).

Prayer Point 2: The second point Jesus makes in the prayer He taught His disciples is about the sacredness of the Lord's name. His name reveals His character. The word of God reveals several names of God. He is called Adonai (Lord), Elohim (God), El Shaddai (Nourishing God), El Elyon (Most High God), Jehovah[2] Jireh (Lord our Provider), Jehovah Nissi (Lord our Banner – the one who fights our battles), Jehovah Shalom (Lord our Peace), Jehovah Tsidkenu (Lord our Righteousness), and Jehovah Rapha (Lord our Healer) and other names. If you forget any of these names, always remember the name that is above every name – Jesus. His name is hallow (holy) and should be respected with the utmost honor. Demons tremble and flee at the name of Jesus Christ. Diseases are healed by the power of Jesus' name. Miracles are wrought by the power of His name. Become familiar with His name and do not be afraid to call upon His name in prayer. There is no effective prayer without the name of Jesus Christ.

Prayer Points 3 and 4: Jesus makes a third point in the model prayer. He says, "Thy kingdom come." The Lord is our king who has a kingdom in which all believers are citizens. His kingdom

---

[2] Jehovah is the English name used to translate the Father's actual Hebrew name of Yahweh [YHWH]/

Chapter 7 - The Model Prayer of Jesus

expresses His rule, His sovereignty, principles, and will. He desires His kingdom to be revealed upon the earth. We have the responsibility of walking in His principles by knowing His will and the way He does things. This segues unto our fourth point of His will being done on earth the same way it is done in heaven. The Bible clearly tells us that we can "prove His good, acceptable and perfect will" (Romans 12:2). God's will is His purpose, plan, and desire. It's what's on His heart and mind. When you pray for the Lord's will to be done, you are really asking God to reveal to you what's on His heart; what He would love for you to do.

Our relationship with God, knowing the power of His name and character, and understanding His heart and will, and desiring to implement it on the earth, is prayer's priority. Everything else is secondary and will be accommodated when it becomes a priority for you. That is why Jesus said, "Seek ye first the kingdom of God and His righteousness and all these things shall be added unto you" (Matthew 6:33). The things we need and desire are just as important to God as they are to us. However, His will has to be just as important to us as it is to Him. These can coexist when they are prioritized.

Prayer Point 5: Jesus goes on to pray, *"Give us this day our daily bread."* After our hearts are aligned with His heart and will, we can craft our prayers with our earthly necessities. We can petition the heavenly Father about the things that are necessary for our natural existence.

Bread (or food), as Jesus puts it, was merely an indicator of His awareness of things we need to sustain us in this life. We need daily resources for life and ministry, and we should petition every need before our heavenly Father. It will be difficult to function on earth without certain resources made available to us. We pray to the Father because He knows how to direct resources our way to meet our need even if He has to perform a miracle to get it to you.

<u>Prayer Point 6:</u> *"Forgive us our debts (trespasses) as we forgive our debtors (those who trespass against us)."* Another thing we need from God for our everyday life is *forgiveness*. Forgiveness is pardoning someone who offends you or letting go of the offense of others. We all have sinned (and still do) and need God's forgiveness. And He does just that – forgives us of our sins – "He is faithful and just to forgive us of our sins and to cleanse us from all unrighteousness" (1 John 1:9).

All of us are imperfect. Even the most seasoned of saints offend others. Just as we appreciate being forgiven, we should likewise forgive the mistakes of others. We forgive others when we let go of resentment and give up any claim to be compensated for the hurt or loss we have suffered. The Bible teaches that unselfish love is the basis for true forgiveness, since love "does not keep account of the injury" (1 Corinthians 13:4, 5). Jesus said for us to pray for our forgiveness as we forgive others. Forgiving others isn't an option if we desire God to forgive us. Forgiving others is beneficial. It helps us to remain pure in our hearts. It helps us to remain solid in our relationship with God. And believe it or not but it also helps our physical health. When we pray this prayer of forgiveness there are two things you want to do:

1. Specifically name the sin that you want God to forgive you of.
2. Specifically name the people who hurt you that you are releasing from their indebtedness to you.

Chapter 7 - The Model Prayer of Jesus

Prayer Point 7: Our seventh prayer point in Jesus' model prayer involves deliverance from temptation (and evil). A temptation is *an urge to do something wrong (sin)*. It is *a luring away by your [carnal] desires*. Temptation is actually an evil attack from the opposition. The attack doesn't really appear as an attack because it often comes as something so attractive. However, it appeases our carnal nature – that part of us that displeases God and fights against His will.

Temptations also can come in the form of trials or difficult situations that threaten your life, your peace, your joy, your sanity, your health, your family, your finances, your future, etc. It is not so appealing. Jesus is telling us to pray so that we want fall victim to these attacks. We should pray God's strength and endurance to be victorious over these threatening situations. When you pray you should petition God about all of your needs and all of the things that are coming against your life and faith.

Prayer Point 8: Jesus made it a point for us to end our prayers with praise and honor. We must not end our prayers with our petitions. Let's remember always that the main purpose for prayer is relationship with God. So, we need to always put a praise on our prayers. Let's always use our conversation with the Father as an opportunity to give Him thanks and to tell Him what He means to us. "Thine is the kingdom, and the power and the glory forever." Everything belongs to Him. When we end in a doxology (praise) we are just showing Him how grateful we are that He allows us to be a part of His great plan and that we recognize his sovereignty as well as his goodness toward us.

Chapter 8
Effective Praying

"As is the business of tailors to make clothes and cobblers to make shoes, so it is the business of Christians to pray."
Martin Luther

It is one thing to pray, but it's another thing to pray effectively. When I use the term, "effective praying," I am talking about the kind of praying that produces results. One thing I encourage believers to do is to make a prayer list with specific, targeted requests. Apostle Paul says, "Make your request known unto God" (Philippians 4:6). Be specific when you petition God. Don't pray aimless prayers. Don't just make up stuff because someone told you that you must pray for an hour! Be specific and intentional with your words when you pray. Communicate with the Father candidly and honestly. We can come to His throne of grace "boldly." This basically means that we can be open, honest and upfront with our request. He promised that we will receive "mercy and grace to help us in the time of need" (Hebrew 4:16).

In this chapter, I will identify and discuss eight (8) key scriptures that will help you become an effective-praying believer.

THE EFFECTUAL FERVENT PRAYERS OF THE RIGHTEOUS
James 5:16-18

"Confess your faults one to another, and pray one for another, that ye may be healed. The effectual fervent prayer of a righteous man availeth much. Elias was a man subject to like passions as we are, and he prayed earnestly that it might not rain: and it rained not on the earth by the space of three years and six months. And he prayed again, and the heaven gave rain, and the earth brought forth her fruit."

In this passage of scripture there are several points that we must highlight. As we mentioned before, Jesus made it a point to let us know that we should pray for our sins to be forgiven. Apostle James confirms that here as he gives us his intake on effective praying. The Lord wants our hearts healed and whole. And here, James adds another element – not only confess our faults (sins) to God but *confess them to one another*!

True revival can take place where there is a nonjudgmental environment. If the enemy can get us judging one another and gossiping about our brother's sins instead of covering them in prayer, then he will cause us to not trust one another enough to ask for prayer in our most vulnerable area of life. Without this brotherly trust, we may never get the interceding prayers we need because we will conceal our struggles from our brother. No one may ever know what you are going through inwardly or emotionally until you confess it. So, find a trustworthy brother in

Chapter 8 - Effective Praying

the Lord who you can confide in or an accountability partner who can challenge you to a life of wholeness and celebrate your victory over sin.

We need to initiate creating the right house of prayer that has a No Judging Zone, a safe place for confessing our faults. According to apostle James, effective praying involves our ability to confess our sins to one another – that we may be healed, especially inner healing from guilt, shame, mental and emotional wounds, etc.

There are certain prayers that you may not receive an answer for if you pray about it on your own. You may need to "touch and agree" with your brother. The Bible says that "one can chase a thousand, but two can put ten thousand to flight." You get rid of faults by confessing them. You can't explain away your fault or make an excuse for your fault, but confess it. "He who conceals his sins does not prosper, but whoever confesses and renounces them finds mercy" (Proverbs 28:13). Don't conceal your fault – confess it. Effective praying begins with the confessing of faults – to God *and* to one another.

Apostle James says that the kind of prayer that a righteous man prays *avails much*. These prayers that avail are *effectual* and *fervent*. The Greek word *"energeo"* is used here for effectual and it means "active, operative; working." It's where we get the English word *energy*. He also uses the word fervent which means "very hot, passionate or a growing burning passion." The kind of prayer that can produce results is an active, passionate conversation that a believer has with God.

Another key element in this equation is that James says the person must be *righteous*. Simply put, righteousness is right standing with God. In order to be in right standing with God, you must first become *born again* through faith in the redeeming blood of Jesus Christ. Afterwards, you yield your life to the lordship of Christ in purity of heart and a lifestyle change that follows sound biblical principles. Righteousness can position you to be able to pray effectively.

Here, I believe James is referring to experiential righteousness rather than positional righteousness. Positional righteousness is what Jesus did to place us in right standing with our heavenly Father. Experiential righteousness is when a person applies godly principles from the word of God to his daily life. The word of God is actuated and exemplified in his life and character. It is faith acted out. Through your lifestyle show the world that you believe. Living by faith is needed for effective praying.

James gives us an example of a righteous man who prayed fervently and produced results. This man was the prophet Elijah. He says that Elijah was a man tempted just like us and had weaknesses just like we do, but he prayed <u>earnestly</u>. Elijah's "earnest" prayer was a living model to what James meant by "effectual fervent" prayer. To be *earnest* not only means to be *serious and sincere*, but it also means to be *"intensely determined."* Effective praying is praying with an intense determination to see God answer your passionate request. Elijah communed with the Father with great passion and with great determination until God moved in great power.

This is the kind of prayer that can move mountains, shut the mouth of lions, heal the sick, raise the dead, and cause strongholds to fall flat. Elijah prayed that the heavens would not produce rain for three and one half years. God honored the prayer of this

Chapter 8 - Effective Praying

righteous man and shut the heavens up until Elijah prayed for the heavens to release rain again. Here is a man who underwent trials and adversities just like us, yet he prayed intensely enough where God moved upon the elements on his behalf. Imagine, you can pray fervent prayers like Elijah and experience the hand of God moving on your behalf. Don't limit what God can do through your prayers. Yes, He wants to use you. I've witnessed blind eyes opening, deaf ears hearing, the lame walking and demons being cast out of people because of intense, fervent prayers being ushered up to the Father.

CLEAN CONSCIENCE (HEART)
1 John 3:20-22

"For if our heart condemn us, God is greater than our heart, and knoweth all things. Beloved, if our heart condemn us not, then have we confidence toward God. And whatsoever we ask, we receive of him, because we keep his commandments, and do those things that are pleasing in his sight."

One great truth to keep in mind when we pray is that God is omniscient – He knows all things, especially the matters of the heart. Apostle John shares with us that if our heart condemns us, if our hearts are not aligned with the will of God and we are experiencing active guilt from besetting sins, God knows it. We can fool others by trying to display an outward demeanor opposite of our inner disposition, but we cannot fool God. He's "greater than our hearts and knows all things." The Lord desires truth in the inward parts. He is more concerned with what's going on inside you than your outward performance. He wants them to match up. A just balance is what the Lord loves. Thus, the Lord works on our hearts. "It is God that is working *in* you both to will and to do of His good pleasure."

He wants to get us to a place where "our hearts condemn us not." If our hearts don't condemn us, then we gain *confidence* in God. This confidence is an inner knowledge of an authentic connection with the Father, a deeper level of realization of a living relationship with God, and what He will do for His children.

Apostle Paul often mentioned serving God with a *clear conscience* and a *pure heart,* or a *heart unfeigned.* He knew that his inner life matched his outer life. He had confidence *toward* God. He had a living relationship with God. There was an experiential connection with the Divine Being, Yahweh Elohim. In fact, Paul was so confident *toward* God that he questioned anyone, "What can separate me from the love of Christ?"

Apostle John says that when our hearts do not condemn us, we have confidence with God and "whatsoever we ask we receive of Him." Here, we see the benefit of having our hearts pure and our consciences clear and clean. We can receive from the Father whatever we ask for. That sounds like answers to prayers! That's effective praying.

PRAYING HIS WILL
1 John 5:14-15

"And this is the confidence that we have in Him, that, if we ask anything according to His will, He

Chapter 8 - Effective Praying

heareth us: and if we know that He hears us, whatsoever we ask, we know that we have the petitions that we desired of Him."

Apostle John reveals another key element to praying effectively, that is, praying His will. Simply put, God's will is his purpose, plans and desires. God's will is what's on his heart. It's what He is interested in.

John says that when we ask [pray] according to his will *He hears us*. This means that He gives special attention to our request because our request is centered around his will for our lives. You may ask, "How can I know His will?" This is where the study of God's word comes into play. His will is revealed in His word. And more specifically, we must become more accustomed to his voice. The Holy Spirit lives inside every believer and is committed to comforting us and revealing God's will to us. He promises to teach us and guide us into all truth. The Lord gave us his Spirit so that we can know His will concerning us.

To ask things according to His will, we must pray His word. We also call this the prayer of confession, not the confession of sin, but confessing what God says. When we pray God's word, we are not reminding Him what He said; we are essentially letting Him know that we agree with what He says. This gets His attention. If we have His attention, then we know He hears us. John says that if we know that He hears us, then "whatsoever we ask, we know we have the petitions that we desired of Him." This is effective praying, because we will have whatsoever we ask of Him.

ABIDING IN CHRIST
John 15:7-8

"If ye abide in me, and my words abide in you, ye shall ask what ye will, and it shall be done unto you. Herein is my Father glorified, that ye bear much fruit; so shall ye be my disciples."

Charles H. Spurgeon wrote,

"If you want that splendid power in prayer, you must remain in loving, living, lasting, conscious, practical, abiding union with the Lord Jesus Christ."

Abiding in Christ is having a living union with Christ, being consciously aware of your relationship with Him and His indwelling presence, and having conversations with Him throughout the day, every day. Jesus also says that His word must abide in us, too. Part of this living, daily fellowship with Him is the study of His word. As mentioned before, the study of God's word helps us to hear His voice more clearly in prayer. Prayer and the word of God are like two wings on an airplane. Just as the airplane needs both wings to fly, we, too, need prayer and the word of God for faith to function adequately.

When we abide in Christ, He promises, "ye shall ask what ye will, and it shall be done unto you." When we abide in Christ, He promises to answer our prayers. We must ask ourselves whether anything is hindering us from a daily, living union with Christ, marked by frequent prayer and a consistent intake of His word.

Chapter 8 - Effective Praying

Abiding in Christ is "unbroken" fellowship with God. The more you have consistent, unbroken fellowship with the Father, the more you will begin to see great results in your prayer life.

Smith Wigglesworth, a mighty evangelist and revivalist who had great miracles demonstrated in his ministry, testified of his prayer life. He said that he seldom prayed for more than thirty minutes, but never went thirty minutes without praying. Now that's abiding in Christ. That is effective praying.

The Bible records that the prophet Daniel would kneel and pray three times each day (Daniel 6:10). He did so even in the face of impending danger.

During one particular season in Daniel's life, all the top political leaders throughout the Persian/Medes kingdom conspired together to force a decree upon the entire land. The decree stated that not one single person could petition (pray to) any God or man for thirty days except for King Darius. Whoever is found guilty of petitioning any God will be cast into the den of lions.

Daniel, having knowledge that the decree was signed and enforced, still went into his house and into the chambers where the windows were open facing Jerusalem, knelt down and prayed three times a day "as he did aforetime." Daniel made up his mind that no one would hinder his daily conversations with God. They found Daniel praying and making supplications to his God, and arrested him and threw him into the lions' den. Early the next day, the king hastened to see what had become of Daniel after being fed to lions. God had delivered Daniel by sending an angel to shut the mouths of the lions (Daniel 6:22), and no hurt was done to him because he believed in his God (Daniel 6:23). Now that's effective praying!

We are told that if we abide in Christ, if we have this daily, living union with Him, that we will *bear much fruit*. Jesus says that our fruit-bearing glorifies the Father (John 15:8). Not only do we get results through effective praying, but effective praying also glorifies God. If you want to glorify God, get to praying.

PERSISTENCE IN PRAYER
Luke 18:1-8

> *"And He spake a parable unto them to this end, that men ought always to pray, and not to faint; saying, there was in a city a judge, which feared not God, neither regarded man: and there was a widow in that city; and she came unto him, saying, avenge me of mine adversary. And he would not for a while: but afterward he said within himself, though I fear not God, nor regard man; yet because this widow troubleth me, I will avenge her, lest by her continual coming she weary me. And the Lord said, hear what the unjust judge saith. And shall not God avenge his own elect, which cry day and night unto him, though He bear long with them? I tell you that He will avenge them speedily. Nevertheless when the Son of man cometh, shall he find faith on the earth?"*

Jesus was frequently concerned that his followers pray continually to accomplish the Father's will for their lives. The main point of

Chapter 8 - Effective Praying

Jesus' parable is that for prayer to be effective, we must be persistent. We learn several things about effective praying from this parable:

1. <u>Men should always pray</u>. We should be tenacious in our desire and discipline to communicate with God. The Apostle Paul admonished the church at Colosse to pray "steadfastly" (Colossians 4:2) and the newly planted church of Thessalonica to "pray without ceasing" (1 Thessalonians 5:17). This does not mean to stop doing everything else in life so that you can go into some prayer closet and pray for 24 hours. Rather, it means to pray recurrently on all sorts of occasions throughout the day.

2. <u>Do not faint</u>. Don't give up or lose heart when it comes to prayer. We must be patient when our answer to prayer does not come speedily or instantaneously. We must continue in prayer until the answer comes. We must remain consistent in our requests. Remember, consistency is the key to breakthrough. A wall does not break from one hammering of the chisel. It takes multiple hits. Keep hitting the chisel until the wall comes down. Keep praying until you get the desired result from God.

3. <u>Recognize what is rightfully yours</u>. In this parable of the persistent widow, she recognized that she was wronged, unfairly mistreated or that someone took something that rightfully belonged to her. And she went to the judge to plead her case. When you go to the Father, our great Judge, know what is rightfully yours or know what was promised to you that the enemy is trying to withstand. The great Judge has the power to vindicate you and give you what rightfully belongs to you.

4. <u>Understand you have an adversary</u>. We must always realize that nothing is going to come to us easily. The reason why is because there is a real adversary to our faith. It is his nature and responsibility to block our blessings and attempt to hinder everything that rightfully belongs to the heirs of salvation.

5. <u>Cause trouble when you pray</u>. The wicked judge said that the widow "troubled" him, and it was because of her "continual coming." Her persistence forced the wicked judge to make a decision because she was constantly in his presence, crying out to him about her case. Jesus said that our God (our great Judge) will avenge his own elect that cry out to him day and night "speedily." In other words, He will answer those who pray persistently more readily than we think. Our persistence in prayer is effective because we know that no matter how long it takes, God will answer us. We just have to trouble Him and stay in His presence until He decides that He's got to do something on our behalf.

6. <u>Know that Jesus sees persistence in prayer as *faith*</u>. Jesus asked the question, "When the Son of man comes, shall He find *faith* on the earth?" By asking this question, he was literally likening the widow's action of persistence in going before the judge with faith. Our persistence in crying out to the Father is likened to faith. He is looking for this kind of faith – persistent prayer faith – when He comes.

THE PRAYER OF AGREEMENT
Matthew 18:18-20

"Verily I say unto you, whatsoever ye shall bind on earth shall be bound in heaven: and whatsoever

Chapter 8 - Effective Praying

ye shall loose on earth shall be loosed in heaven. Again I say unto you, that if two of you shall agree on earth as touching any thing that they shall ask, it shall be done for them of my Father which is in heaven. For where two or three are gathered together in my name, there am I in the midst of them."

We have such an awesome power when we can come together in agreement. That is why Satan fights unity so hard. He knows that once we start agreeing on earth, the Father shall bring to pass what we ask for. There are four ingredients that must be enacted in our prayer of agreement in order for the Father to materialize it on our behalf. These four ingredients include:

1. <u>Binding and loosing together.</u> To bind (Gk. *Deo*) means to put under an obligated commitment, and to loose (Gk. *Luo*) means to free from an obligated commitment. We must make ourselves obligated if we are going to be effective in praying with one another. We are obligated to uphold our end of the agreement. This is similar to a business contract, where we must be responsible for doing everything we agreed to in the framework of our agreement. The only way out of that agreement is by being loosed from it by the other person. When we come into agreement with someone in prayer, we must be committed to praying with them until we see what we are praying for materialize. Too often, we abort the prayer assignment and divorce ourselves from one another before the things we committed to ever come into fruition. The prayer of agreement takes patience and endurance.

2. <u>Agreeing</u> (on earth). To agree means to be like-minded and supportive. We must find someone of like mind who wants to ask God for something you both believe is the will of God for your lives together. The Prophet Amos denotes, "How can two walk together except they be *agreed*?" (Amos 3:3, emphasis added). Not only should we be like-minded, but we should also support one another if we are going to agree on something. Your prayer partner is very important to certain things coming to pass in your life, and that person will need your support just as much as they need to support you in life.

3. <u>Touching any *thing*</u>. The word "thing" here is *pragma*, which means *concerning what is to be accomplished; business, matters, or affairs*. To touch any *thing* means to settle or resolve what you are willing to accomplish together.

4. <u>Asking together</u>. Once you know what "thing" you ought to accomplish together, you must *ask* God for it together. There's a little bit deeper meaning to this as well. The literal Greek word that Jesus uses here for ask is *aiteo*, which not only means to request but also to desire or crave for. I believe that when we request something from God together, both parties should have a passionate desire for it come to pass. Find someone who will be just as passionate about the very thing that you want to see God materialize in your life, and pray consistently together with them until you see it come to pass.

THE EFFECTIVE PRAYER FORMULA
Mark 11:22-24

Chapter 8 - Effective Praying

> *"And Jesus answering saith unto them, have faith in God. For verily I say unto you, that whosoever shall say unto this mountain, be thou removed, and be thou cast into the sea; and shall not doubt in his heart, but shall believe that those things which he saith shall come to pass; he shall have whatsoever he saith. Therefore I say unto you, what things soever ye desire, when ye pray, believe that ye receive them, and ye shall have them."*

This passage of Scripture is a key element to effective prayer. It reveals the posture your faith must take once you decide to verbalize aloud what you want God to do for you. You must:

1. <u>Have faith in God</u>. This means to trust the Father wholeheartedly. The Lord never turns away a person who depends upon His name, His character, and His power. *"Trust in the Lord with all thine heart; and lean not unto thine own understanding. In all thy ways acknowledge Him, and He shall direct thy paths"* (Proverbs 3:5, 6). When we call upon Him, we must *believe that He is* (Hebrews 11:6). He is trustworthy. He is all-powerful. He is a loving God. He is able to do exceedingly abundantly above all we ask or think (Ephesians 2:20). He is able to do unimaginable things for us.

2. <u>Whatever you desire, you must *say* it</u>. God requires for us to open up our mouths and say exactly what it is that we want or need from Him. He moves upon what we *say*. He himself brought the world into existence by what He said. There is creative power in speaking words. When we speak words of faith to Him, He goes

into creative mode and creates exactly what we need manifested in our lives. We shall have what we say.

3. <u>You must not doubt in your heart</u>. This is a vital and pivotal part of this formula. Doubt can be a major hindrance to answered prayer. The New Testament Greek word used here for doubt is *diakrino,* which means "to separate or to withdraw oneself from; to oppose." When we say or release our prayers to the Father, we must be careful not to sever ourselves from it by using words and actions that are in contrast to what we said. Be careful what you say after you pray. Don't walk away from what you say! Keep saying what you originally said until it comes to pass.

4. <u>You must *desire* what you are praying for</u>. Psalm 37:4 tells us that the Father *"shall give thee the desires of thine heart."* This comes after we "delight ourselves in the Lord." There are two things to consider here. First, we must desire what we say. It'll be hard to pray for something you don't necessarily want. Second, we must check to make sure we are delighting in the Lord. Do you take great pleasure in His nearness, His love, His word, His righteousness? Some prayers aren't effective because we seem too bored with God. He wants us to say prayers born out of a delight for Him and his will. You will always have His attention and answers when your desires spring from delighting in Him.

5. <u>Believe you already received them when you say it</u>. The last component of this formula is unique. Jesus says, "Believe that ye receive them, and ye shall have them." How can I have something that is not there? Aha, but perhaps it is there. It is created in the spirit realm before it is manifested in the physical realm. You must use your spirit man to receive them before they physically materialize. One way of doing this is by using your holy

Chapter 8 - Effective Praying

imagination and visualizing in your mind the Father literally handing you the very thing that you request of Him.

A messenger angel told Daniel that from the very first day he set himself to pray to the Father for understanding and clarity for "a thing," his words were heard and that he was sent to give him the revelation, that very thing he requested (Daniel 10:12). Your words reach the Father's throne as soon as they are released from your lips. And His answers are delivered the moment He hears them. Now, imagine your answers are literally on the way. Can you visualize it? Just give it some time, because like Daniel, there may be some satanic opposition fighting hard for you not to have it (Daniel 10:13). Just as the archangel Michael helped the messenger angel to break through the satanic interference, you will receive angelic help until you tangibly possess in this physical realm what you already received in your spirit.

Jesus promises that the result of using this effective prayer formula is "ye shall have them." When you take this posture as you pray, God will surely manifest tangible results on your behalf.

PRAYING WITH THANKSGIVING
Colossians 4:2

"Continue in prayer, and watch in the same with thanksgiving."

As mentioned earlier, for our prayers to be effective, we must be persistent. Here, in Colossians 4:2, it is reiterated, "Continue (be steadfast) in prayer." But this time, the Apostle Paul adds another element. In our frequent communication with our heavenly Father, we must make sure it is done with "thanksgiving." I believe the reason for thanksgiving is to keep us in the right attitude and to appreciate what God does for us.

> "In everything *give thanks*: for this is the will of God in Christ Jesus concerning you" (1 Thessalonians 5:18).

Giving thanks in everything is God's will for us. Other Scripture verses that point out that we should be thankful as we pray are:

> "Be careful for nothing; but in everything by prayer and supplication with thanksgiving let your requests be made known unto God" (Philippians 4:6).

> "And whatsoever ye do in word or deed, do all in the name of the Lord Jesus, giving thanks to God and the Father by Him" (Colossians 3:17),

> "I exhort therefore, that, first of all, supplications, prayers, intercessions, and giving of thanks, be made for all men" (1 Timothy 2:2).

Chapter 9
Praying in the Holy Ghost

"But ye, beloved, build up yourselves on your most holy faith, praying always in the Holy Ghost."
(Jude 1:20).

I discovered in my walk of faith that praying *in the Holy Ghost* (or *in the Spirit*) is one of the most effective ways to pray, if not the most effective. This includes the ability to speak in an unknown language or "praying in our heavenly language." Depending upon a person's doctrinal persuasion, they may not clearly identify with this type of prayer, or they may teach what it means to pray in the Spirit altogether differently. I cannot escape the teaching of this particular type of prayer, mainly because of my personal experience, which has produced undeniable evidence and manifestations over the years. I encourage you to learn this method of praying and incorporate it into your daily prayer routine.

When we pray in the Spirit, we are praying by the enabling power of the Holy Spirit. We look to Him to inspire, guide, energize, sustain, and help us in prayer (Romans 8:26). Praying in the Spirit involves praying with one's spirit (1 Corinthians 14:15). Praying with our spirit is where it gets complicated for those who wish not to believe in the ability to pray in other tongues. I will explain my personal perspective of this subject matter.

Building an Effective Prayer Life

In the above-mentioned Scripture, the Apostle Jude gracefully challenges us to build up our most holy faith. There are several ways that we can build up or strengthen ourselves in the faith. We can build ourselves up in the faith by constantly studying and taking in the word of God (Romans 10:17, 2 Timothy 2:15; 3:16-17), committing to the tutelage of the fivefold ministry and those who watch over your souls (Ephesians 4:11-13, Hebrews 13:17), by remaining in the sphere of God's love for us and love for people (1 John 4:7-21), and continual fellowship with the body of Christ (Hebrew 10:25). There are other ways to build up ourselves in the faith as well, such as serving, giving, and looking for the blessed hope and appearing of our Lord Jesus Christ. Jude, however, mentions another essential way of building ourselves up in the faith: by praying in the Holy Ghost (or in the Spirit). Apostle Paul mentions this to the church of Ephesus, "Praying always with all prayer and supplication *in the Spirit*" (Ephesians 6:18, emphasis added).

The Apostle Paul also teaches this powerful truth to the church of Corinth. He says,

> "For he that speaketh in an unknown tongue speaketh not unto men, but unto God: for no man understandeth him; howbeit *in the Spirit* he speaketh mysteries" (1 Corinthians 14:2).

Let me point out three specific truths Paul reveals to us in this verse:

1. When speaking in an unknown tongue, you are not speaking

Chapter 9 - Praying in the Holy Ghost

to men. You are speaking to God. When you are praying in tongues, it is not for any other person or being to understand but God.

2. When speaking in an unknown tongue, you are "in the Spirit."
3. When speaking in an unknown tongue, you are speaking mysteries (or secrets). I love this truth because it reveals to us that when we are praying in the Spirit, we are speaking secrets to God. When we pray in our heavenly prayer language, it is like speaking an encrypted, coded language which only God can decode. This frustrates and confounds our enemy because he cannot discern what's being said or what the Father might do in response to our encrypted prayer.

Apostle Paul later tells the church of Corinth that when he prays in tongues, his spirit is praying, but his mind is unfruitful (without understanding). He says, "I will pray *with the spirit*, and I will pray *with the mind* also" (1 Corinthians 14:14, 15). Thus, when we pray in tongues or in the Spirit, our spirit man is praying. When we are praying in the Spirit, our mind is unfruitful. You are not going to know what you are saying to God. Not having knowledge of something always makes it difficult for us humans. The unknown always takes a deeper dimension of faith and trust in God. Let me remind you that His love surpasses our intellect (Ephesians 3:19), His peace surpasses our understanding (Philippians 47), and His judgments are unsearchable, and His ways are past finding out (Romans 11:33). There are just some things that you will not figure out with your own finite intellect. This is where faith and trust in God have to kick in.

Jesus assured the disciples, *"If a son shall ask bread of any of you that is a father, will he give him a stone? Or if he asks a fish, will he for a fish give him a serpent? Or if he shall ask for an egg, will he offer him a scorpion? If ye then, being evil, know how to give good gifts unto your children: how much more shall your heavenly Father give the Holy Spirit to them that ask Him?"* (Luke 11:11-13). If you are asking anything of the Father, whether through the natural or in the Spirit, He is not going to give us something evil in return. He will give us better things than our natural fathers could ever give us. So, be at ease when it comes to praying in the Spirit and not having any understanding of what you're saying. Remember, it's encrypted, and only the Father can interpret it.

In Romans 8:26, the Apostle Paul shares another truth about praying in the Spirit:

> "Likewise the Spirit also helpeth our infirmities: for we know not what we should pray for as we ought: but the Spirit itself maketh intercession for us with groanings which cannot be uttered."

As the entire creation groans and travails because of fallen humanity and awaits the coming of the Lord, who will make all things new, the believers also groan within as we await the redemption of our bodies (since our spirits are already redeemed). While we await full redemption, our spirits grieve living in a sinful world, experiencing imperfection, pain, and sorrow. We groan for the glory to be revealed and for the privileges of full sonship (2 Corinthians 5:4-10). Likewise, the Holy Spirit, who is in us, helps

Chapter 9 - Praying in the Holy Ghost

us with our infirmities (weaknesses). The word "weaknesses" is the NT Greek *astheneia*, meaning "an inability to produce results." Not only does the Holy Spirit help us by giving us strength to endure trials and temptations, but He also helps us to produce results that we cannot normally produce in our own human capacity – God-kind of results. This is a deeper purpose of grace.

The Spirit helps us by interceding for us. The intercession of the Spirit is according to the will of God (Romans 8:27). He prays what needs to be prayed when we don't know what else to pray for from a natural standpoint, "for we know not what we should pray for as we ought" (Romans 8:26).

When the Holy Spirit intercedes for us, he groans. When we release the groaning of the Spirit within us, it comes out as an inarticulate sound, a sound too deep for words. This inarticulate sound is the Spirit praying the will of God for us. The Father, who searches the hearts, hears the groaning and knows that it is coming from the Spirit and that it is an urgent request for Him to intervene on our behalf with power from on high. The Spirit may be requesting more strength to withstand temptation, a breakthrough in a long-lasting crisis, healing in our bodies, wisdom from above, favor among men, or an overdue blessing or miracle from on high.

Be confident that praying in the Spirit and allowing the Spirit to make intercession will produce God-kind of results. Paul says that it will be beneficial for us, *"And we know that all things work together for good to them that love God, to them who are called according to His purpose"* (Romans 8:28). Praying in the Spirit works for our good. It helps us in our conformity to the image of His Son (Romans 8:29). It's for our good, but for His glory.

Conclusion

Now that you have read and picked this book apart it is time to commit to a life of prayer. It is time to go from reading to *doing*. "Whatsoever he *doeth* shall prosper" (Psalm 1:3, emphasis added). The Lord is waiting for you to *do* prayer so that He can prosper you. You now have the tools to build an effective prayer life. Jesus gave us a model prayer to build upon. Do not let any excuses or any doubts hinder you from praying persistently and fervently. Make those important appointments with God and keep them. When you become consistent in your prayer life, you will become closer and more intimate with the Father, and your life will never be the same as you witness the countless miracles and blessings that God will do in answer to your petitions.

Through your prayers, the world will be impacted, souls will be saved, lives will be changed, miracles will happen, revival will take place, and the good news of Jesus Christ will advance on the face of the earth. Let me pray for you:

Father in heaven, I thank you so much for the opportunity to encourage and challenge fellow believers. I pray that as they reposition their lives and make prayer a priority that you will do incredible things in response to their believing prayers. Let their faith increase and anoint their life with the oil of joy. As they abide in you, allow them to bear much fruit and live the abundant life that you promised. For this I give you praise, honor and thanksgiving. In Jesus' name, I pray. Amen.

About the Author

Since 1993, Bishop Palmer has been preaching the word of God. He founded his first church in 1995 in Annapolis, Maryland. In February 2000, he was consecrated to the episcopate in the Church of God in Cleveland, Tennessee. He is currently the senior pastor of Kingdom Celebration Center in Odenton, Maryland, and the presiding prelate of Kingdom Alliance of Churches, International (KACI).

During his tenure as bishop, he has raised up and ordained ministers of the gospel, covered and planted churches not only in the United States but also in Kenya, Uganda, and India. He has also traveled to foreign countries to assist with missionary work, including preaching and teaching the gospel of Jesus Christ at Leadership Conferences, feeding thousands of hungry families, distributing toys and books to children in need, and building a support base that helps finance orphanages and children's nurseries in East Africa. He has also done missionary work in Mexico, El Salvador, and Jamaica.

Bishop Palmer enjoys serving God alongside his beautiful wife, Pastor Barbara. They share bundles of laughter and life experiences with their son, Randy; his wife, Kimberly; their three grandsons, Katriel, Khairi, and Kairo; and their twin granddaughters, Rylei and Ravyn.

www.ingramcontent.com/pod-product-compliance
Lightning Source LLC
Chambersburg PA
CBHW071756080526
44588CB00013B/2262